ONCE UPON A TIME

The plight of my very own struggle and how I
overcame the stigma of my past....

ONCE UPON A TIME

The plight of my very own struggle and how I
overcame the stigma of my past....

Inspired By True Events

By Michael Marshall

Marshall, Michael 1965 –

ISBN 978 1519311863

Autobiography/Prison-Ministry/Counseling

Cover photo by Reggie Thompson
Book Cover Design by Justin Young /Firstborn Designs
Editing by Rhonda Ross/A New View 4U

DEDICATION

TO PRISONER RE-ENTRY

I would like to dedicate this project to the prisoner re-entry process by sharing God's redemptive power through my own testimony. It is my purpose for living today. My inspiration for publishing this book is to positively impact the hearts and minds of individuals who have been stigmatized by their past and inspire them to put their pasts behind them while embracing HOPE. My endeavor is to help them embrace a new beginning through a genuine relationship with Jesus Christ while allowing the practical and spiritual principles to work together for their GOOD!

PREFACE

For the last 23 years I have worked to better myself through a new found relationship with my Lord and Savior Jesus Christ. I have learned a great deal about myself through it all and have concluded that hard work and determination is the key to a life I can be proud of living. Today I stand humbled by God's grace that has allowed me to further my education and to become intricately involved in community initiatives that service youth, ex-offenders and homeless citizens.

This book is my personal testimony, and my way of saying, "Please forgive me for the negative impact of my contribution on the communities in which I was involved during the"80's". I take full responsibility for my past lifestyle and for the direction my life had gone. Please allow the words in this book to serve as my sincerest apology to anyone and everyone that was impacted by my criminal behaviors. Almost 23 years ago, and much earlier, I made some costly mistakes that I regret, but I can't change the past. By no means is this book intended to glorify a life of crime, drugs and violence. However, it is to help change the path of our younger generation while also bringing encouragement to all those who continue to seek a way to escape their own madness.

TABLE OF CONTENTS

ACKNOWLEDGEMENTS

Heavenly father I come to you as humble as I know how. I confess my sins, those known & unknown. Lord, you know that I am not perfect and I have fallen short many days of my life, but I just want to take time out to say "Thank you" for your Grace and Mercy and how you restored my life ...Lord you deserve all the praise and honor.

I have had more on me sometimes than I feel like I can bear. I am so thankful for mercy and grace making the load lighter for me each and every day throughout this journey. I would like to take this time to pay tribute and homage to those fellow travelers who have positively impacted my life along the way.

To my angels that God has blessed my life with, Carolyn and Terrell, thank you for being such an amazing part of my Once Upon A Time reality. I love you to the moon and back.

A Special thanks to my uncle, Pastor Cordell Carter of Higher Ground Outreach Church, the most positive examples in my life as a child and beyond. Thank you

11

for setting a standard of righteousness to be followed as a God fearing man.

To the Indian Creek Therapeutic Community and St. Bride's Correctional Center – Ms. Robinson, Jackie White, Jennie Aminson, Dr. Buck, Mr. Piccolair, Charles Owen, Lori Perkins, Mr. Griswell, Jackie Taylor and Juanita Mills-Griffen– THANK YOU!!! Your guidance, direction, and consistent support through my transition from incarceration to this present day have been my energy empowering me to start life anew.

I thank you God for my siblings, nieces and nephews, family, and friends, including my Facebook friends, former and present colleagues who have been there for me through it all. You know who you are. There are so many, I can't even name them all. I would like to give special thanks to some individuals who truly made a difference in my life knowing and unknowing.

To The Urban League of Hampton Roads – Thank you for giving me my First Opportunity. I realize that you didn't have to believe in me, but you did! Laurel Wilcox, a former Urban League employee, thank you for your professional and spiritual encouragement, and personal advice that was always deeply cherished and respected. Ms. Edith White and Yvette Young, your support and kindness are truly appreciated and heartfelt.

I would like to thank Don Scott who gave me a chance in spite of it all. You definitely impacted my life in so many ways.

I would like to also pay tribute to Cynthia Thompson. Cynthia has been a key influence in my life. She helped me professionally when we worked together at the Norfolk Department of Social Services. Most of my leadership attributes are a direct result of our working relationship during that time. She always believed in me and through it all she has remained a great friend and colleague.

Reggie Thompson, my brother, my friend, thank you for your constant encouragement and example of integrity. Thank you for your photographic magic.

Alphonso Albert, my mentor and inspiration, you are the example I follow throughout my career path. Much appreciation for your diligent work and effort in the Second Chances Programs in restoring formerly incarcerated lives and helping others in the community.

Dr. Kirk T. Houston, Sr. Pastor of Gethsemane

Community Fellowship Baptist Church, thank you for the very strong spiritual impact you have had on my life while attending your ministry for over 8 years. Your passion for the redemption of ex-offenders continues to bless me.

Much love to my extended Carter family.

To my business partners, Rhonda Vaughan and Wanda Brown from First Opportunity, LLC.

To Dr. Denise Biron, as you rest from your labor, I acknowledge you as a "Re-entry Angel". Thank you for your iconic work and dedication to the restoration of those who found themselves trapped in societal turmoil. Truly I was a life impacted by you.

Michael Paris, thank you for being a great friend over the years. Blessing to you for your pioneering efforts in assisting those in re-entry to secure employment over the many years I have known you.

To Gina Tanks, Sheila London and Ninette Adams, Sandra Peters and Denise Williams, thank you for your encouragement and support during my time at Norfolk Social Services (KRA) VIEW Program.

To Leslie Wilson, my spiritual mom, who prayed for me throughout this journey, I love you eternally. I thank God for placing you all in my life throughout this journey from my past, to my present, and into my future. It has not been easy, but God made a way when some said I wouldn't make it.

Sherese Hargrove, words cannot fully express how much I appreciate your contribution of time and effort in being my sounding board as well as my second set of eyes and ears. Thank you for assisting me with bringing the book together as a whole. I am forever grateful.

Dearest Mom, Grandma, and to my
Beloved Sisters:

Although, you all are gone I still feel your presence each and every day. I pray that I have made you all proud of the man I've become. Mom and Grandma, don't worry about me because I have God's word hidden in my heart just as you taught me. Thank you for instilling in me the word of God daily and for that your love and prayers never fell on deaf ears. I've kept my promise and I'm alright now because I'm back with God! I humbly dedicate this book to each and every one of my Guardian Angels, if not for your love and God's grace and mercy I would be **NOTHING**. I Love You All!

I thank you God for guarding my heart and my mind over the years and for protecting me throughout all of my transgressions. I thank you most of all Father for not giving up on me. For I know that this blessing that you have bestowed upon me is not by happenstance but it is orchestrated by the works of your mighty hands. And with the fruit of my lips I will forever give your name all the honor, all the glory and all the praise for it belongs only to you! I'm thankful for all who have been positive motivating forces in my life. I recognize there will always be naysayers but I will raise up a standard against them and use them as my footstool and as a source of encouragement to keep me rooted and grounded in you. I no longer have to worry because I know to whom I belong and that no weapon formed against me shall prosper. Heavenly Father, I graciously commend this project back into your hands for all that I have ever needed you have provided and for that I am eternally grateful. Nothing can ever separate me from your love. I Love You Lord!

Your Son,

Michael Marshall

INTRODUCTION

For I know the plans I have for you," declares the LORD, "plans to prosper you and not to harm you, plans to give you hope and a future. Jeremiah 29:11 NIV

It was on a Saturday morning in late June that my *"Once Upon A Time* "journey would begin to unfold. After many attempts to schedule an interview appointment, I was finally able to synchronize my schedule with Ms. Williams. We met at Starbucks on Military Highway.

Since I had never had an encounter with Ms. Williams in person, I was not really sure what to expect. I found myself overwhelmed with the idea that someone would be willing and interested in collaborating with me on this project about my life. I immediately sensed her positive energy that instantly connected us. This synergistic vibe helped me to become more relaxed and at ease with the whole interviewing process.

The interview began with Ms. Williams complimenting me for my hard work and perseverance. "I know it hasn't been easy over the years, but your hard work towards change", she said, "is paying off". She went on to say that she had heard some great things about me. I politely responded that the journey had been hard but looking back, it was obvious that the experiences I had encountered and the lessons I had learned made me the man I am today.

She then commented on the outfit I was wearing, which looked like it was something straight from off the block. I was wearing white T-shirt, khaki pants with Adidas sneakers and a NY Yankee fitted cap. I grew up watching older dudes, but mostly my older brother Tony and my Uncle Tee-Tee Carter (RIP), who would wear similar fashion trends. I remember when they used to wear Khakis pants and white sneakers (preferably Chuck Taylor All Stars).They always had a handkerchief in their back pockets. That was style and trend of dudes growing up in Ida Barbour Projects during the 70's. I explained to Ms. Williams that I felt like I was representing the urban look from back in the day.

As I sipped on my cup of decaf coffee, I noticed Ms.Williams shuffling through a few index cards with questions on them. After organizing herself, she asked me if I was ready to allow her to enter my head. Her witty gesture made me laugh and I was overcome with a blend of peace and humility. I felt a certain sense of gratitude that someone would take the time out of their busy schedule to interview me about my life. What a privilege it was to share with her how I was able to make it through all the pitfalls that life had dealt me. I looked up at Ms. Williams, and said, "Yes, I'm ready". She said, "Okay, so let's get started. My first question:"

Q. So, Michael how old are you now?

A. I'm 36 years old, and counting, but I feel much younger.

Q. What type of jobs have you worked in the past?

A. To be honest, I worked for summer youth programs and at Farm Fresh, bagging groceries, when I was about 16 years old. I hadn't worked most of my early adult years other than odd jobs.

Q. What has been your favorite job up until this point?

A. Working as a volunteer with the Youth at the Urban League. This was the best job to me mainly because I was able to help those that

19

were in need. My life was so parallel to the people I was serving that it motivated me to take this volunteer opportunity personal. After all, I could relate to them on many different levels which created a very passionate approach to my work.

Q. What High School and or College you attend?

A. Well I went to Manor High School, but I was put out of school in the 10th grade behind an incident involving weed.

Q. How would you describe your life in less than ten words?

A. I have been highly favored by God and blessed.

Q. What is your Motto?

A. A dream is just a dream until you start doing something to make that dream a reality.

Q. What's your greatest fear?

A. Not finding true love and my soul mate.

Q. With whom in history do you most identify?

A. I would say Dr. King. I have learned so much from his powerful speeches. W.E.B Dubois, Harriet Tubman, and President Obama. All were great leaders that never gave up the fight.

Q. What do you regret the most?

A. I think about my earlier life decisions that led me to do so many stupid things that always ended up in disappointments is what I regret the most.

Q. What is your greatest achievement?

A. Well besides building a relationship with the Lord and my kids, I would have to say when I was presented an award at Norfolk Department of Social Services through the VIEW Program for an act of kindness towards this elderly man just coming home from prison with no money, clothes, shelter or official identification documents. I helped him get his disability check, secure stable housing, and reconnect to his family.

Q. What is your greatest flaw?

21

A. I have flaws just like any other person and I come up short sometimes. I have to remind myself to be careful about working too hard and not taking time out for family and friends. Sometimes, I think I am very hard on myself.

Q. What is your best quality?

A. My heart is compassionate towards others and I love helping those in need.

Q. What would you change about you?

A. I honestly can say I like me today. I wouldn't want a different me. I'm an improved me and I am very comfortable in my own skin.

Q. What traits are most noticeable about you?

A. I'm a sociable guy who enjoys talking to people. From what I have been told, I have a distinguishing look and my salt and pepper hair is noticed by most at first sight. I tell people that my grays showed up early

Q. What is your biggest pet peeve?

A. Ignorance and judgmental people.

Q. What is your favorite occupation?

A. Substance abuse facilitation is what I enjoy doing the most!

Q. What type of diet do you have?

A. Well I started off eating only fish, chicken, vegetables and fruits for over 28 plus years. For the past two years, I went to eating only fish, tofu, and soybean products.

Q. What is your favorite song(s) or musical? artist?

A. Well I grew up around the old school Kats, Marvin Gaye, Barry White, O'Jays, and Temptations Curtis Mayfield. My newer artists are Will Downey, Kem, and Jonathan Butler. When I was younger I listened to RAP. My favorites were Biggie, Tupac Mace, NWA, and Public Enemy. Now my gospel favorites are Fred Hammond, Donnie McClurkin, Juanita Bynum, and Martha Munizzi, William Murphy-just to name a few.

Q. What are your favorite movies?

A. Ten Commandments, Cooley High, New Jack City, Training Day, The God Father, The Book of Eli, I grew up watching Bruce Lee and Karate movies. Every weekend we went to the "Capitol "a movie theater that was on Effingham St. in Portsmouth.

Q. What would you like to say about how you were inspired to write this book?

A. I began writing my story in a jail cell just to pass the time and to help me cope with the everyday stress and tension I was experiencing; it was like therapeutic to me. I didn't know almost twenty plus years later the name "Once Upon A Time" would come to me. I have changed my book title over and over.

That day was an eye-opener for me. I walked away from that interview knowing that I have a story to tell and there were truly people who could benefit from it.

CHAPTER ONE

IDA BARBOUR PROJECTS

Ida Barbour Public Housing is where my life's story all begins. I'm the 5th child of seven siblings: three brothers - Tony, Ronald (aka JUG) and Leonard (aka Bolo) and three sisters - Carolyn, Sheila, and Yvette. It was the early 1970's and we were growing up in the hood as normal kids, full of innocence, purity, and hope. We had dreams just like all other kids. We were being raised by a single mother who preached Jesus faithfully up until the day she passed.

My sister Carolyn is the oldest and was like the protector of us all. She was known for her aggression when it came to protecting her family. I heard she had gained a reputation for not backing down from a fight. She definitely was and still is the essence of a big sister with a motherly entwine. Sometimes I think she always felt more like a mother than a sister to us. She most definitely gets the highest level of respect from all my siblings including myself.

She got married at a very early age and moved away with her husband Linwood and daughter, my first born niece Trice to Colorado Springs. He was someone she met earlier on in her life. He went into

25

the Army right out of High School. I only remember her leaving to move out. After moving away I don't remember how often we would hear from her, but I believed she always checked on us. I was just so young that I don't recall a lot.

My oldest brother Tony was like our hero. He was a great baseball player and could pitch a ball like no other. I learned that my brother's father had taught him how to handle a baseball and he became good at throwing it. I remember my mom taking us to watch my brother play. I knew early after watching my brother that I would play baseball just like him. He was our only role model and hero.

As I grew older, it was still always a dream of mine to one day play baseball professionally. Neighborhood games were the highlight of the community. Families would gather from far and near to cheer on their favorite team. I can remember the uniforms we had to wear. They weren't like these new fancy uniforms worn today. They were hot, wool and itchy. My brother's favorite number was fourteen. He wore that jersey proudly and became one of the most talked about athlete for his athletic ability. Often times he would pitch no hitters. His talent didn't just stop there; he was also a dynamic quarterback in football. My other brother, who goes by the name Jug, was not really interested in sports. He had a niche for drawing. He was good at it. My brother Leonard, aka (Bolo), was the youngest of us all. He probably wouldn't remember too much about mom. He wasn't even three years old when she passed away.

What I remember about my younger sisters is that they were always under momma and they hardly could do anything. They often played this game called hopscotch right in the very front of the house which was a very popular game. They would draw this diagram on the ground and jump around inside the blocks. As I got older, I realized the game was just as important to the girls then as electronic games are to the younger generation today. My sisters would play that game from sun up to sun down, if they could. It was the best game next to hide and seek which everybody liked mainly because that was the opportunity to seek out your most liked person.

Although we were living in the projects, we were a happy family with whatever we had, which wasn't much. We always had food to eat and clothes to wear. I remember when those holidays came around; my mom would always go out of her way for Easter Sunday. She would buy new clothes for everybody to wear to church. During those days in the 70's, Easter Monday was like another holiday that was celebrated in the hood. You could count on getting a new outfit to wear to the movies, a tradition I think mostly happened depending on your community. Honestly I don't remember having a lot of bad experiences growing up in the hood. Truthfully speaking, we probably didn't realize we were poor until we moved away from there.

We never knew about anything better at the time. As young children I believe we were all happy with us as a family. My mother was a very spiritual person and believed in the Bible and the Lord with all her heart up until the day she died. She never complained to us or said anything against the Lord. As a matter of fact, she would always encourage us to love, honor and obey the Lord and keep him first in our lives. She was always reading the bible to us, and it was customary that we all watched the Ten Commandments together every Easter.

My mom did not play when it came time for church. It was mandatory for us to go to church just about every Sunday, or whenever that church bus was running; I mostly remember that old Greyhound looking bus coming to pick us up on Sundays. We had to go to church all the time. I'll never forget New Community Church of God In Christ. That's where we went faithfully for years! During those days we were in church all day. There was no luxury of having the option of attending different services like it is today.

From sunrise to sunset we were in church. We couldn't wait to get back home. We just wanted to be home so we could go outside and play with our friends before the street lights would come on.

I remember my mom always calling for us to come into the house. As soon as those street lights came on, it was over. She could call our names like nobody's business. I think all the moms had that call going on when it was time for you to come in the house.

I know things must have been challenging for my mom and the money must have been tight because my brothers and I all slept in one room and all my sisters in another room. For some reason I remember the gathering place being in my mom's room. Although we may not have had a lot during those days, nothing much could replace the love we felt from our mom. Her love over shadowed anything else we may have been experiencing at that time.

When I think of her today trying to raise seven children on her own, it becomes obvious to me that she had a very hard struggle trying to provide. Our ages ranged from 2-15 years old. Growing up with six other siblings and a mother who was very ill with breast cancer was one of those things I will always remember. We all lived in a three bedroom brick house that was known as public housing.

The vague memories I have of my mother are mostly centered on the love she had for God and his word. Nothing stands out more to me than her ongoing prayers and the word of the Lord she would speak into our lives. My mother was the oldest of all her siblings and had a great childhood. She was raised in a stable household and neighborhood (Lincoln Gardens) in Portsmouth.

I don't remember much about my mom other than what I have learned from my older siblings. I was told by my brother Tony that moms would do whatever she could to provide for us sometimes running all her credit cards up just so we could have nice things. He said she was a very loving mother of her children.

My brother use to share how he would dream of getting momma out of public housing one day by playing professional baseball. He was very close to her. I believe he was so hurt about mom's illness that he couldn't focus anymore on sports. We didn't really have a male role model at that time that could have stirred my brother on another path. It would be my sister Carolyn who would enlighten me on the struggles mom would have endured. She shared life events about my mom that I would be too young to recall. Based on the information she shared I figured that something must have happened in my mom's life that caused her some type of emotional pain. I just can't imagine what that could have been. Regardless of what it could have been if anything, I thank God for her short life and the fact she introduced us all to the Lord Jesus Christ. God knows she did her best; after all there were seven of us and only one of her.

It's so weird, but I can still feel her in my heart even to this very day, as though it was yesterday. It's been said that love is deeper than the grave meaning that our love can go down into the grave and take the sting out of death! I heard a minister preach that before and it has stuck with me. He explained that love runs deep and it never ends even at death I had never heard it put quite that way. I guess maybe that's why I felt her love all these years although she wasn't here and her flesh went away, but our love for her never died.

Mom had been sick for many years with cancer. I can remember when one of my mom's brothers came by to visit her. He was driving this nice pretty blue car, a Fleetwood Brougham made by Cadillac, what a pretty car it was to us. We were young kids and had not seen that type of vehicle at least not close up.

My mom's brother was very close to her, as he was the second oldest. I had never seen my uncle (Bro.) before, but his name was like power in the family.
When I first met my Uncle, I was very fascinated because of the car he was driving. He always drove

Fleetwood's Brougham. He was always dressed from top to bottom wearing nice clothes, and lots of gold jewelry. I remember him always giving us money when he would stop by our house. I think we all wanted to be like him.

CHAPTER TWO

MOM'S CANCER TAKES A TURN FOR THE WORST

My mom and little brother Bolo

In 1975 mom's illness turned for the worst. I can remember my grandma moving in with us for a short period of time. One of the most significant moments I can remember is the day grandma had all my siblings come into the room with my mom. I never forget when she allowed us to see the hole in my mother's chest where the cancer had completely eaten through her flesh. This image has never left my mind to this very day. It was like the size of a golf ball. Grandma would use peroxide to clean the wound followed by stuffing her wound with cotton balls.

We would stand around the room, not really understanding what cancer was. All I knew was that mom was always in pain with a gritting of her teeth. She would be so medicated with all sorts of pain killers. I guess the only treatment was to attempt to keep her comfortable. It wasn't unusual to see her nodding her head as the medications put her in a relaxed mood.

By now grandma was providing everything for us and making the day to day decisions. She was the best care taker anyone could have asked for. My mind often wondered what it must have felt like for my Grandma to see her child slowly slip away into the transition of life into death. It became obvious to us that our beloved mom just was not able to care for us as she had in the past.

It seemed that everything just happened to us suddenly. The next thing I can remember was that mom was home with us one day and the next day she was admitted to the hospital because she was getting worse. I remember the very moment that it became painfully clear that we may not see our mom at home again. It was winter of 1975, actually two days before

Thanksgiving, Grandma had visited momma as she normally did and returned back home to care for us.

We ate dinner and went to bed. Later that night, well into the late hours of the night, a phone call came in. All I can remember is the loud crying from Grandma. She woke us all up to tell us the news that mom had passed away. My siblings and I were crying and hugging each other. We had nobody but our mom. I think no one can imagine losing a parent at that age. It's the worst feeling you could ever experience. She would leave us at thirty-five years old. Mom spent a lot of her adult life very ill, from what I can remember. Grandma had been there by her side through the entire ordeal. She was a very strong woman and in my opinion, and so was my mom.

I know the love my grandma had for mom, her oldest daughter, was unconditional and there was nothing that she wouldn't have done for her. Although I couldn't feel my grandmother's pain, after all I was only nine years old then. But now, I really understand what it's like to care for someone who is dying right before your eyes. There's nothing you can do about it but pray that God will give you the strength to carry on. After all, my grandmother's faith in the lord was the very foundation my mother was built upon.

1 Corinthians 10:13 declares that God will not put more on you than you can bear. Also David says to Solomon in 1Chronicles 28:20 do not be afraid or discouraged for the Lord my God is with you, and he will never leave you or forsake you and will be with you always even until the end. These were the type of scriptures that my grandmother, my siblings and I could get strength from during this very difficult time into the present moment.

My brother, Tony, was used to being with our mom and by her side through everything. When mom died I believe a piece of all us died with her. Based on the conversations I've overheard in the family, I know that life stopped for him when mom passed. It was a period of grief that sent him down another path in life.

One of the most important things, to this very day, that I thank my mother for is how she planted JESUS in us. I remember people always quoting Proverbs 22:6 Train a child in the way he should go, when he is old he will not turn from it. My siblings and I always had that working on our side. On the other hand, whether we practiced it or not is a different story. The fact still remains that God has been our source of survival throughout our earlier years and beyond.

CHAPTER THREE

THE HOME GOING SERVICE

My mom now had gone home to be with the Lord, as the church folks would say. We, as a family, were preparing for the funeral. This part of my life was very painful and numb. It's like I really don't remember all the details. I believe we were all expecting the worst, but hoping for the best.

Thinking back when people passed on during those times, the funeral director would put this black bulletin looking sign up with a light on your front door. It would have the white lettering with all the information about the deceased person. I was scared of that sign for some reason and I would always see it posted at other people's houses. However, when they put it up at our house I was just terrified of this sign to the point I didn't want to come to my own house.

I can still visualize all the people sitting around talking about past stories, sharing the good and not so good times about mom. On the day of the funeral we all rode in the family car, all seven of us. Grandma had us all dressed up in nice clothes. We were all together, probably one of the only times we would ever be together again for the rest of our lives although we didn't know it then.

During the funeral I was so scared that I hid behind someone to keep from viewing my mom's body. I just didn't want to look at her and I never did. I remember my brother, Ronald, jumping out of the car trying to jump into the ground with my mom. He was stopped by somebody and put back in the car. He really has never been the same anymore from what I know and see in him. Looking back into that time period of our lives, being so very young and trying to make sense of it all was difficult.

I know it's a painful experience that I will never forget. We found it hard to deal with and I believe we automatically drew closer to each other. Although like any siblings you have your disagreements. We always had a close bond with each other. It was understood that it was just us now, no mom or dad but us. We only knew that true love that came from Mom.

To lose your Mother as a kid is unfathomable and it was the worst pain I've EVER felt! As an adult I know that her transition was necessary to rid her of the excruciating pain she experienced daily. I seek solace in knowing that her suffering is over and I will see her beautiful face again. God loved her best and he endows me with the strength to know that her love surrounds me each and every day and I'm thankful.

CHAPTER FOUR

THE FAMILY MOVES TO LINCOLN GARDENS

My Grandparents

Shortly after my mom died we moved to Grandma's house in the Lincoln Gardens section of Cavalier Manor in Portsmouth. Grandma's and Granddad's goals were to keep us together although she received many requests from others to adopt us. Some were relatives and others were non-relatives that wanted to adopt us but Grandma held on to us tight.

Although she had already raised her own family of about seven, which I know she must have been physically, emotionally and psychologically tired, but she pressed her way through it. She was a candy lady for many years and the neighborhood loved "Mrs. Carter". She was a very strong minded woman and though she was tired, she was determined to keep us together.

39

My grandparents lived in a three bedroom house and had limited space for six kids, nevertheless, they made it happen. We continued to share rooms as we had always done. However, living in Lincoln Gardens was such a new experience from the life we were used to. The new environment, I must admit, was exciting as a young boy. Having a back yard to play in was something that always made me happy because I loved to play football and baseball. It was cool to have all our friends around Grandma's house. Back in the hood you didn't have a lot of grass in your yard to play anything. As a matter of fact, you didn't even have much yard.

It was scary at first, because "wow" did grandma have a different set of rules. We would come to realize that mama's rules were simple, but they were strict and consistent with Grandma's. There wasn't any jumping on beds, running around the house, playing hide and seek and staying up all times of the night. You had real rules. In reality, we had fun. There was a time and place for everything. Grandparents were grandparents in those days.

I felt my life was finally moving up when I got to the Manor. I felt somewhat middle class in my mind maybe. It was so much different from the projects. The adjustment was still hard but we eventually adapted to our new environment and life seemed to be wonderful.

I must say life with my grandparents was good. I absolutely loved Cavalier Manor, it was cool. I met many friends from the neighborhood. I had many friends who were my age. We use to have the time of our lives. I often ran with a small crew of guys even though I had a huge extended circle of friends from around the way. Those were the days of clean fun, not all this killing for no reason and hurting each other over petty matters as you see things played out today in the media.

Grandma enrolled us all in school, and life seemed to be back to normal for the most part. I use to think about my grandmother is getting older and maybe she doesn't have the energy like she use to in order to raise seven more children, but she did and I never heard her complain about us being there she was an amazing woman and she always found time for humor. We all loved grandma but there were times I felt sad and thought about my mom.

It's just the truth of the matter that no one could replace her. If you have ever bonded with your mother, you would understand. I knew Grandma loved us unconditionally, but it's something about your mother's touch, and nothing or no one can fill the place in your heart for her.

That's the heaviness that never goes away; life just couldn't ever be the same as we knew it. For a very long time I reflected on the big question to GOD: WHY did she have to leave us? It was like something we cared about so deeply was just taken away in an instant, just like blowing out a candle.

I remember my grandfather added additional rooms onto the house at some point. He was a great man in his own way. He was a very hard working man who believed in an honest day's work. My grandfather didn't say much but he was full of knowledge and wisdom. He taught us a lot through his actions and he had certain expectation and if you didn't follow those expectations and or his rules you were definitely not going to live under his roof long. My grandfather wasn't a hands-on type of man, but he led by an example of what a young man should become.

I saw him work tirelessly, watch T.V., and play his guitar at the church faithfully. He enjoyed going to church. He was a simple man, but very wise. One thing for sure, he had a close grip on his money and it wasn't going to leave his sight. He believed in keeping all his money close to him. When I think back, I don't think he even used a bank. He was just "old school", but it worked for him and he never wanted for anything. The most important thing I can say about my Grandfather is that he put a roof over our heads.

My brother and I would often joke as we got older about some of the phrases grandfather used. One of his favorite lines was God bless the child who got his own.

We all knew it would come a time for us to separate, but the experience of dealing with separations after separations was a bit overwhelming. I think back when my oldest brother, Tony, was the first to leave. He was about fifteen years old. He had dropped out of school and with my grandfather's strict rules about living under his roof he had little to no choice but to leave. If you weren't doing anything with your life you weren't going to stay there. Tony left without looking back and began living with his girlfriend, and eventually got married to her.

The second separation came when my brother Ronald was sent to live with uncle Cordell. We were very close in age and shared a lot more in common than Tony. We had done mostly everything together in our younger years. He was now out of my life for the most part .We would still see each other at Church "New Community COGIC Pastor Ted Thomas, respectfully who's now Bishop Thomas.

This is when church on Sundays became a must for us, because it was a way for us to see each other, and we looked forward to that time; not that Ronald had much of a choice because uncle Cordell went to church faithfully. So he had no choice but to be there. On the other hand I was there whenever I could be.

CHAPTER FIVE

I'M IN A NEW YORK STATE OF MIND

Life was appearing to be normal, but it wasn't. My father somehow after all these years came around and wanted to get me and my sister to live with him in NY. So out of nowhere, I was uprooted and moved to NY leaving all my real friends here in Virginia. I was in the middle of a school year. I was bound for the city without any reason or true cause. This is something I came to resent to this very day.

My sister Sheila and I went to live in New York with our dad .The man I knew as my dad shortly after getting us to New York would later abandon us. I don't know if there were some issues with his girlfriend which led him to take us to his mother's house, but she didn't know us which was an awkward experience. Don't get me wrong, she never mistreated us. However, the impromptu drop off was not welcomed. That would be the last time I saw my father for more than 30 years.

Times were tight for his mother. She didn't have enough resources for me and my sister. It became obvious that she was unable to provide for us. My sister and I found ourselves living from place to place.

Eventually my sister would move in with an older guy. She was accustomed to taking care of us when we were very young. She was a young lady with an old soul. She always tried to protect me and keep me from getting into trouble when I was living on the streets in New York.

She tried to get me to come with her but I refused. The streets soon became my home. I began to live on the streets at thirteen. My sister would often check on me. She would give me money whenever she could. I was very street wise and had a hustling mentality that I had picked up from watching some of the older family members when I was younger. I never resorted to that when I was in VA. Now in New York, with basically no one but my sister to help me, I went for what I knew.

I found my first hustle selling snow cones. I worked for this older kat who I believed was in this motorcycle gang. He was cool though. I would learn later that his snow cone business was a front for his drug selling. I would make a little cash and buy clothes and food. In addition, some of my street friends I met had other hustling products that were much more appealing to me because they were making more money. I wanted and needed that fast cash in my life, so I thought. It became a fast track for me all the way. I was introduced to marijuana and I thought at the time it was the best thing happening for me. By now I was sleeping outside and not even going to school.

It was never meant for me to stay in New York long term but I got trapped there by default. That's the hand that was dealt to me. It all became survival for me. I was just trying to put food in my mouth. I grew up really fast learning all the tricks and trades of the underworld. By the time I left New York, I felt like an expert in surviving on the street.

I remember not having a place to go and nobody to guide me. I made it the best way I knew how. I know my sister often times worried and feared for my safety. She really cared about me and always encouraged me to go back to Virginia. But by now I felt no need to go back. There was nothing for me in Virginia anymore. Hopelessness began to fill me and I wanted to give up. I can remember sitting in the train station crying because I felt like I had no one to care for me.

We were all young but loved to be in that street life. I was so caught up in the day to day things I forgot I was just a young kid running around with no guidance who needed to be back in school. I often thought about my other siblings back home. Life had become so fast track for me I didn't have time to cry or worry anymore. All I knew was survival. There were other times I would pray and ask God to help me and my sister.

I always believed in God when I was out there in the streets, but I just didn't have anyone to guide me through. One of my ways to escape my reality and pain was baseball games. I would go to Yankee Stadium as often as I could, even with no money. I would sneak in the stadium just the way my cousin had taught me. I loved to see the bright lights on the field. It was something about the lights I loved.

When I looked up into the skies I felt such a sensation that took me out of this world. That's when I would imagine myself pitching that ball or I could see my brother in my mind on that field. I used to love when they would have bat day, ball, jacket day, and all these other give-a-ways. I knew the schedule and most of the players, like Reggie Jackson, Thurman Munson, and Cat Fish Hunter, Mickey Rivers, just to name a few. Life was so good at the games. It was my only way of escaping my reality at the time.

I believed my sister contacted Grandma in Virginia.
She must have felt that my life was in jeopardy.
After a confrontation I had with some Spanish guys.
The next thing I knew, I was on my way back to Virginia as per Grandma's orders.

CHAPTER SIX

MY RETURN TO PORTSMOUTH

I was sent back to Virginia and was enrolled in Waters Junior High School. I was doing well playing on all the sport teams: football, baseball and basketball. I became a bit popular for my athletic abilities. Being a left-handed pitcher gave me an advantage and I loved baseball. I was a gifted running back in football. All my coaches often pushed me hard because they saw potential in me. Most of my coaches were always concerned about my behaviors. I was traumatized by my experience, still damaged and borderline doing what was right from wrong. All the negativity I had been exposed to while in the city trying to survive was taking its toll now that I was back in Virginia.

There were times when I was playing sports and I had no family support. I could look over to the sideline out into the stands but no one was there cheering for me, other than teammate families. I wanted most of all the support when I came back from New York and I made the baseball team.

One day my brother Tony came to my JV football game. That must have been one of the happiest moments of my season. We were playing Cradock at home and I saw my brother on the sideline. I was filled with excitement that I actually ended up showing off and got the team a penalty for something stupid. Often times coaches would ask me about family support but I would always avoid the questions about my family and what inspires me about sports so much. Occasionally I would talk about my oldest brother's athletic abilities and how I used to look up to him.

My siblings and I ended up back together living with one of my aunts. She was a disciplined person who had high expectations for her nieces and nephews. Living with her taught us how to maintain a clean home and self-control. It was challenging but she was able to fulfill her duty to her sister.

We were all moved back to our grandmother's house because my aunt moved from the apartment. We were getting older and things began to change. My brother Ronald and my sister went out on their own journey to seek life for themselves.

Times were hard for us emotionally and we often talked about our mom to each other. We relied on each other and would have benefitted from some counseling. We cried together, we hugged one another and as young as we were we found a way to show our love for each other in our own way. I can remember wanting a bicycle but with money being tight I had no other options or means to get one. My brother Ronald built one for me from old bicycle scraps around the neighborhood. I was really glad to get that bicycle and looked so forward to riding it after school. Regardless of what the most important thing that came out of this was that we were all living together the five younger siblings. My older sister and brother were now living their lives and didn't have much contact with us. We would often think about them and missed them dearly.

My sister Shelia would leave Virginia again and go back to N.Y. We had been in N.Y. together earlier in our lives. She was so fascinated that she went back because of this man she had met, I believe. However, I didn't know this would be the last time I would ever see my sister Sheila. She was murdered by someone in New York.

I think most of the family had a hard time with her sudden death. However, we managed to make it through. Devastated I began to lose interest in school because life had drained me emotionally because of all the ups and downs. I just didn't really care anymore. I began to wonder why God would take all my family away from me. I didn't understand back then that death was a part of life and we all must make that journey.

Although, we never found out who the perpetrator was we had an idea of how she ended up dead. The most hurting part about this for me was that I wasn't in New York with her and she was found alone in an empty building. She just didn't deserve that to happen to her. Her body was flown back to Virginia. She was put to rest. I was so hurt about this that nobody could find me the day of her funeral. I was so emotionally distraught, I was determined that I was not going to attend another funeral. I just disappeared because I couldn't take it. It had always been a fear of mine to see someone in a coffin. I lived with this tragedy in my heart most of my life.

CHAPTER SEVEN

GOOD-BYE MANOR HIGH

I lost my focus on everything and began to hang out with a few known thugs. Everybody thought they were troubled youth destined to be confined and weren't going to do anything good with their lives. But one thing about me, I was always a leader and I never followed anyone besides my family. I really wasn't fitting in with the crowd, but I became the best actor you could have been. I was back to living a life in the street much like my old lifestyle when I was in N.Y.

I was on my way to the 11th grade, but I didn't make it once again my bad choices would have consequences. Grandma was so disappointed. Nothing else mattered to me except living a street life style. I grew to accept that this was how my life was going to be. The streets had become where I would spend my future. I was convinced I would probably die at an early age. I was so lost in that world. The ugly truth revealed it was filled with traps waiting for me to fall in and I did.

Another painful experience that I had to live through was when my baby sister would end up in foster care. I missed her so much. I cried inside every day for her for a while. It was like a silent cry. I was screaming for help, but no one ever heard me. I felt like something inside of me had died as I was screaming for help. I never got any counseling or help for the pain I experienced. I learned how to cope with my pain in so many ways that led me to making so many bad choices. Not having my baby sister around anymore was one of the worst feelings I could have ever experienced. I thought, *what else could happen*?

Confused and distraught again, I made connections with the weed man in Ocean view. I began to save my money and purchased more weed weekly. I was determined that I would survive by any means necessary. In addition to purchasing more weed, I began to tap into the market of selling rolled up joints at a discount price. I had customers of all ages ranging from my age up into adults, some twice my age.

My little weed operation began to grow and I began to purchase even more marijuana and started occasionally smoking it sometimes myself. It never became a habit for me. The effects of how it made me feel paranoid wasn't for me, so that was short lived. I thought I was doing big things. I started to buy better clothes. I even purchased this older model car an LTD. I had a few jobs in between all these activities. I worked at Farm Fresh bagging groceries for about six months, but the demand for the weed was paying me more. By now I had stop playing sports, something I loved dearly. I exchanged that for fast money, fast girls and to feel like I was somebody. Eventually I was put out of school permanently.

CHAPTER EIGHT

LIVING IN THE FAST LANE

Me in the fast lane
23 years old

By now life had taken me down so many roads of disappointments, I didn't know which way to turn. I could no longer face the fact of my reality and what life had become for me. I was now about seventeen years old and was hanging out with people twice my age. It was like living a double life. Good guy by day and bad boy at night.

I spent a lot of time at my main man Ray's house (aka Dr. Funk). His garage was our meeting spot where we would sit around and talk about everything.

I don't think he knew at the time all of the things I was going through. He never asked and I never told. We had a real close bond, and I knew he was someone that I could always trust, one thing for sure regardless of what was going on, I could count on getting a laugh from this joker. He was the funniest dude I know, and still is to this very day. We use to play music all night in his garage while talking on the phone with the girls. These were the good old days. Ray aka (Dr. Funk) definitely earned his place in the DJ's Hall of Fame should it ever be one. Another good friend Lil Mike aka Mighty-D, aka Drummer (RIP) Uncle Pen bought him the best DJ system money could buy, it was something out of this world. Mighty-D would get his proudest moment at the Armory Downtown Portsmouth during a battle of DJ's dance when he faced off with one of the all time great Greg from Chesapeake known as "Controller" he also was a magician at the hands of a turntable.

I enjoyed going to Ray's house and I admired his dad a lot. Mr. Sessoms was a good man and set a good example for us young dudes in the neighborhood. He never closed his doors to us and always made us feel welcome in his home. Being at Ray's house is where most of the homies would meet up. I can say it was nothing but brotherly love amongst the crew. It was like home away from home. Although the fellows knew I was caught up in the fast lane by now, and the street life had me going in different directions I would still stop through from time to time, but my life plans had shifted to something totally different. But it was nothing like my homeboys from around the way (Lincoln Garden). It was a bond that we just had no matter what we went through. I think of Eagle Dog who had a Vegas way of style with the dice and he always came ready to play. He could throw a lick on you real fast. There were a lot of us who would hook up from time to time. When we got together it was a good time to me. It was something about the fellas: Speedy, Mack, the Mack Brothers, June-June, Dennis, Perry, T. Epps, the Cherry's, Joel and the West's. It was about having clean fun and finding our way through life. Sure we had our own share of disagreements but it never carried over into something that brought serious violence, harm or danger.

Those were the days where you got into a fight but you went home and nobody died. You might become rivals but there was no killing. You may have to show your courage as a young man. It was a time when it was all innocent and nobody was looking to end your life. Who would have ever thought a lot of our life decisions would carry us into so many different directions that would be disastrous for some.

My life was constantly changing and not for the better. The struggle was real and the downward spiral

I had become entangled in seemed to have been aggressively perpetuating as the days continued to roll by. I could just feel that something bad was about to happen. I had been running with dudes that I normally didn't hang out with. A lot of bad things were constantly happening and I got myself caught smack in the middle of it all.

On a very rainy day, sometime early May, I was walking down Avondale Rd. around the way and was stopped by the cops during school hours. They pulled right in front of me as though I was on the most wanted list. One of the officers immediately jumped out of the car and asked me my name and if I had an ID, then he says where do you live, I pointed in the direction of grandma's house. I'm thinking to myself, I should have been in school, but in all reality I had dropped out. The other officer got out of the vehicle. I knew it wasn't going to be good for me that day. They pulled out these photos and asked me if they could search me, which I gave them permission to do so. I was then told I was being taken downtown for further questioning. I was handcuffed and placed in the back of the police car.

Once downtown they began to question me about the robberies that had taken place in the areas. Somehow I had been implicated in some robberies. I was still a juvenile, so they booked me and I was sent to what was known as (TDH) Tidewater Detention Home. I remember calling home once they gave me a one time phone call. I can remember talking to my uncles and brothers. All I know is that they were adamant that I said nothing and I didn't know nothing. I stuck with that story to the end.

During my confinement, I thought back over my life and where I was headed. I was thinking I may never see the outside again and possibly spend the rest of my life behind bars. I was due to get released after having all of my charges dropped for the exception of one. My plan was to go to college upon my release.

My homeroom teacher from Manor High School supported me and was a character witness during my trial. She often wrote to me, and encouraged me to complete my GED, and I did. I gained about fifteen college credits with her support through NSU who had started a program for offenders.

When I was released, I found a few jobs after a long search. The hours and money were so little. I began to think of ways to get back to a much better place financially. So I started back hustling and working at the same time. That lasted for a while and eventually I stopped going to work. I felt like there was just one dead end job after another. I went back to the street life again. I hated being in that life but I couldn't escape it. I had a quick easy connection from within the family and I knew just about all the hustlers. It was just a matter of me letting the fellows know I would be getting some product and would get back with them, it was just that simple. It wouldn't be weed anymore. I reached out to some other long time friends that I had heard was already out there doing their thing and making money; I was putting the word out that when I get my package we would hook up. What I didn't realize is that things would go to another level. There was no time for playing around. My connection had been doing this game before I was born and was very true to it. This was an entirely different type of clientele than those I was selling weed to. The money was coming in so fast I got a rush seeing it; just as much as the heroin addicts were getting a high from their next fix.

Hustling is a job day and night. I could feel the streets talking to me and If you wasn't on point you could get caught up really quick. There was a lot to deal with, you had the boy's coming to stick you up, then you had the Narcs chasing you all freaking day and night. It just wasn't worth it when I look back over it. But in all reality everybody was trying to get some money, it was definitely a lot to compete with. This once upon time was real for me and every hustler that was living it, for what I see and hear on the News daily nothing has changed about the life style and nothing probably will ever change. I realize people have to change because the streets and hustling wont. Take it from me it's no winners in that type of life, it only brings the same results jail, prison life long addictions and, or death. It's no life I want to see anyone live.

I eventually connected with guys from all over Portsmouth. I knew so many kats from the streets, and It was no denying that. I use to wonder, with P-Town being such a small town, where's all this money coming from. I know every dealer got his proportion, because there was plenty of cash to go around. The stories of some of these kats hustling in P-town like rags to riches, ghetto superstars or whatever you want to call them but they were out there. Some were young and old. You even had dudes coming as far as New York and Miami just to catch some of the action.

During my days on the streets, I had friends and associates from all over Tidewater. These dudes were real people and their names spoke volumes to their personalities. No one used their formal government names just to mention a few like D.L., Lil Willie, DJ, Putt, Big Hank, Peyton, Skint Man, Teddy and Sonny. My homies, like Funk, Bat Man, Lopo, and Prep had a history and there were so many more.

My ace Koolaid, and I had done a lot of hanging out

in our days, he was always dressed to impress, and was most definitely the ladies choice.

Bat Man grew up in Ida Barbour and from what I remember he could play some baseball also. He was a bit older than me. We had not seen each other in years but our paths would finally cross after many years later when I was doing time. Batman was always a likeable dude in my opinion who always kept it real. During the late 80's we hooked up and the rest is not to be told. His mom always looked out for all the fellas and everybody had much respect for her.

Lopo (RIP) was my ace who always had my back and vice versa. We had mad respect for each other. His funeral was one that I couldn't miss. Paying my respect to my partner brought tears to my eyes. He will always be remembered. The most significant thing I learned about my comrade was that he had recently given his heart to the Lord and had been baptized. Hearing that news really blessed my heart.

My man Prep and I met on a summer job through the STOP Organization when we were teenagers. We became friends in the early 80's. Fate would have it that our paths would cross later on in our journey. We have remained friends until this very day. We went through some good and bad times together but the

64

experiences that didn't kill us made us strong.

My homeboy Curtis, who was more like my brother was God sent during the time we first met. Right from the beginning I could tell he was a different type of dude. He wasn't like the guys I usually ran with; for one he was in the Armed Forces and was very organized. The thing that stands out to me the most was his strong work ethic, it didn't matter how late we were out partying this brother would be ready for work as though he never went out. He always tried to steer me in the right direction. He opened his home to me when I was still trying to figure things out with my life. We became close like brothers, but I would often distance myself because I know I wasn't living right. After he married we didn't see much of each other, but we could always count on each other for support.

He had a style of his own. He was gifted with a charm that was out of this world. He had a street smart about him that could catch you by surprise because of his meek personality. He was very wise. He knew exactly when and how to code switch. He always had a plan for everything. We made a lot of "power moves", as he liked to put it.

The fast lane wasn't my life plan, but being as though I chose to live it, I would get full orientation into the world of something that I knew nothing about. My connection is someone who in his own right a living legend in his era. He is most definitely in a class of his own. Our initial meeting was to talk about my role in this operation. He had his own way of doing things which there was no compromising. Often times I had to go through his brother to get deals done because that's just how he made moves.

I had known about him being a multi-millionaire twice, having so much money he had to hide it in the walls. He was accustomed to living a lavish lifestyle from the late 70's up until the late 90's. His circle of contacts would carry him to another level, even making connections with the Oriental's who was known for their product labeled "China White". This was a term used by the street hustlers as a brand of heroin that's most potent. What I was not aware of was the terrible turn of events that this connection would bring to my world.

My connection would put me in the presence of other major drug dealers. I know I always carried several hundred thousands of dollars with me at a time to New York to purchase more drugs. Once arriving in the city, I would then catch a cab to Harlem. We would wait at one of his locations until he received that phone call from someone acknowledging that the transaction was about to happen.

I can remember one deal in particular that I was involved in. We were to meet to carry out a major deal that was set up by one of his female friends. We spent days trying to negotiate a meeting place. We waited days to make this deal happen and were stuck in the city for about a week. We finally got the call. All agreed to meet at the neutral location that had been arranged. I can remember waiting in this room while the deal was about to go down. It was clear that I couldn't be in the room while the transaction was taking place. I couldn't see them entering and nor could they see me.

My connection placed his pistol behind his back. He told me I would be notified when they arrived. He had given me an automatic weapon and told me if anything didn't sound right not to ask any questions just come out shooting. I knew then that I was into some serious stuff.

For the first time being in the game, I experienced a thought of wanting out but wouldn't dare show that to my connection. I was used to dealing with the minor league dudes but this time it was on another level like the major leagues. I was being paid to handle my business. I was making amounts of money that I had never seen in my life. I was so much younger than all the other dudes who were down with my connection. These dudes must have been fifteen to twenty years older than me, but I would gain the respect.

I had always looked up to my connection and I knew he trusted me. I felt like I had earned his trust, and became solely responsible for picking up money from all the locations. It was a real job to him. One day when I was late getting somewhere I was supposed to be, I remember being told that I need to be on point. My connection was against a lot of hanging with crowds and often taught me to be solo in all my transactions. He was always giving me a lesson from Hustling Book 101. I felt like I was in boot camp around this dude. He didn't play and was serious about his business. He was just straight Gangster. He always schooled me about how to survive in the game.

He never forced the drug game or his way of life on me or anyone else, but he would say if you choose to hustle I rather you be down with me. He would give me the laws of the game before anything else, in his own way he was giving me the best of what he knew. As I drifted out there on my own I begin to make a lot of bad decisions that would eventually lead me to using drugs myself for over a three year period off and on. I tried to hide this from my connection, but being the seasoned street wise guy he was, he figured it out, and I was immediately cut off from everything. It was late 1989 I had recently got cut off from my main connect and was trying to get myself back right. I thought about these Dominican brothers I had met a few years ago coming back from New York who actually were staying in Florida, but had ties in Norfolk. I had never done business with anyone other than my connect, so I was very hesitant about trying to contact the brothers but now because I was trying to purchase some drugs in weight I needed them like really quick.

It would be almost a year later that I would try to contact them, but with several failed phone call attempts I had given up. Three weeks later my beeper blowing up, to my surprise it was one of the brothers. I met with them and to my surprise they would agree to what is known as "fronted" drugs without payment. One of the brothers was very specific about his attitude towards being paid for this transaction by saying to me, "Man we don't play about our money". I knew exactly what that meant since I had used similar statements in the past. I wasn't worried about getting the money back because I knew how to move the product. What I didn't know was that so many things would go wrong with the package of drugs.

Trusting others to help me carry this out was probably not the wisest thing to do. Money was mishandled and I found myself having to make other moves to recoup the loss of the money I owed. Not being able to make the pay back, I then sought out another connection to help make up for the loss. So I was introduced to another known major drug dealer also from Norfolk who was operating in Huntersville.

We clicked immediately and shortly after I was moving product with him and things were looking good again, so I thought. I still had unfinished business that I never made good on with the brothers from Florida. So now I became an enemy of theirs and my life was placed in jeopardy. I remember thinking *now how would I protect myself?* I knew in this lifestyle it was either you or them. By now I had become very paranoid of everything not knowing what the outcome would be.

Totally unexpected and unprepared I eventually came across one of the Florida brothers at a service station on Effingham and South Street in Portsmouth. I was pumping gas not realizing what was going on. I was having a conversation with one of my homeboys. He noticed these guys staring at me. He alerted me and said, "Hey man, what's going on with the guy in the Jetta with the tinted windows? He's gritting on us." I turned slightly around and noticed it was one of the brothers I had unfinished business with. He pulled up next to us and said, "What's up Mike?" I had to think quickly. I said, "I just got back in town and was going to call you." He gave me a look that indicated it was about to go down. His friend in the back seat was telling me to get into the car. I noticed the gun in his hand. I realized he could have easily pulled the trigger and it would have been over for me.

All I knew was if I had gotten in that car I would have never been seen again alive. I looked at my homie, and signaled for him to jump on the interstate that was near. I told the brother that I was going to move my car from the pump and park. I finished pumping the gas as they parked on the opposite side of the service station. I acted like I was parking to get into the vehicle. I quickly stepped on the accelerator and sped out of the gas station onto the route leading to 264. I knew I had just escaped my death that day. I met up with my homeboy later to let him know what had just happened.

CHAPTER NINE

DRUG DEAL GONE BAD

Portsmouth was a very small city, but the drugs and most particular the heroin traffic that flowed through you would have thought it's a major city and the violence was just a part of everyday news. It was small compared to surrounding states up North. Portsmouth was a hustler's haven if you asked me. It was very inviting to those coming from other cities.

The streets were rough and there seemed to be no refuge for hustlers on any level. Beyond the danger of fellow hustlers and ballers making their last rounds for the night, there were Narcs to be on the lookout for. One of the most notorious "Narc- man" of them all was a police nicknamed "Tennis Shoe" must say he earned his name honestly during my era. A typical day would consist of him pulling as many hustlers and "wanna-be's" as he could.

On a cold day in January 1991, I got caught between a bad drug deal sort of situation. I remember getting the call that something had happened in a dead end area out in Ida Barbour where everyone came to hang out to hustle or just congregate known as the "Hole". It was never a dull moment there. It was somewhere you could always find whatever you wanted.

After receiving a phone call, I rushed out of the house without thinking. Lincoln Park was my destination. I had to see what was going on; but what happen next would change my life forever. The person who was suspected of stealing "some stuff" from a friend was allegedly fatally shot by someone else who was very close to me.

Although my friend and I had nothing to do with this crime at all, the both of us would end up getting charged with 2nd degree homicide –not as a principle person of the crime, but more so an accessory, however it didn't matter, it was still horrible. I thought I had a break in the case when sometime after the fact, a witnesses would later admit that I had nothing to do with the incident.

By now I was on my way to prison. All I could think of was how to fight these charges. On visiting days all I talked about to my then wife Pinky was my appeals, she would listen with excitement most times. I dedicated my first five years to researching my conviction in the Law Library and appealed my convictions on every level.

Unfortunately I was never exonerated. The feeling of being falsely accused, wrongfully charged and convicted for this crime which I was never implicated or charged for shooting anyone, but rather an accomplice has been a heavy burden to carry over the years. I will come to grips with the fact that I lived a life style of hustling and sometimes you don't know how your ending will be.

When I first arrived at the Portsmouth City Jail I was assigned to a cell in the basement as I waited for the classification process to begin. It would probably be hours before my name would be called, but it didn't matter, all I could think about now, was how could this be happening, me facing these serious charges for something I didn't do. I believe I slept for two days.

Although I was looking at some serious time behind bars, part of me was relieved it was all over. I used to pray to God for direction in my life because I was tired and wanted out of this senseless street life at least that's what I told myself.

CHAPTER TEN

ON MY WAY BACK

For some reason many people think the first thing someone does when they go to jail is grab their bible. Well, part of this may be true, but the reality is; nothing can help you the way the word of God can. When you go to jail the bible is probably the first and only book you would need to read. I had always read my bible, so a few guys I knew from the streets would ask me about things they didn't understand in the word. I'm definitely not claiming to be a bible scholar by no means, but when you have encountered the type of kats I knew from the streets who never stepped foot in a church for the exception of a funeral. I felt honored to share my minuscule knowledge with them.

When I was in the local jail it was the most difficult experience of my incarceration. After waking up the morning after, I was so angry with myself for all the bad decisions I had made. Using my hurt and pains would no longer be my excuse. I had come to accept the fact that I was doing whatever I wanted to do; because I could. I Had made my bed hard, so now I had to lay in it. I had nothing but time on my hand and would spend most days thinking about what went wrong and why.

As I'm sitting on the steel, iron and concrete daily in jail I began to reflect back on how life could have been should I followed another plan, but the thought dissipated very quickly, there was no time to think backwards.

The first dude I came across on the floor was a old childhood friend. He started to run the latest street wire down to me. It had always amazed me how kats in jail would know just as much about the latest happenings on the street than you did, especially when you just recently came from off the streets-well it wasn't hard to figure that out. You have a lot of time on your hands to read the newspaper and watch the news like it's a soap opera.

My conversations were short, and few. All I could think about is how would my life be from here. I had as little communication as possible, at this point the reality was that I could actually be on my way to doing some real time.

Within a few months, I went to court. I was tried, found guilty and sentenced to fourteen years in prison. Truth is, I had been facing so much more time. On my way back to the jail from court all I could think about was my family. I was emotionally sick.

I had recently married. I thought about my wife often

because I knew she couldn't handle this type of time I would have to serve. I earnestly asked her to move on with her life, because there was nothing I could do for her. She would continue to visit me on a regular basis despite the situation, I must say sincerely I appreciated her support and dedication over the many years up until the day I was released.

I was transferred from the local jail after spending three months there. I was happy to leave the jail I needed to get on with my time. The morning they called my name for the penitentiary, you would have thought I had hit the lottery. It's a happy moment when your name is called to leave the local jail, such an experience that only someone who has been there would understand.

When the deputy came down the hall and said "Mr. Marshall, B&B" which is a term often used by the deputies who was informing you that your stay at the jail was over and that you needed to be bagging up whatever personal items you were going to take with you. In my case, I was leaving to go to prison and wouldn't be able to keep much once arriving to the prison. So I left all my property with a good friend. I had met a really good deputy who had a great like for me. I shared with him about my brother who was in the jail and if I could get a favor from him. He knew I wanted to see my brother which would probably be the last time for a many years. He took me on the floor where my brother was on to say my farewell. I remember my brother standing at the bars with tears in his eyes.

We stared into each other's eyes as if we would never see each other again. My brother, Jug, was a very hardened individual. He was without shame and allowed the tears to roll from his eyes making his final statement as I began to walk away "I love you little bro."

I was taken to the waiting area to be transferred. I was ready when the deputy car pulled up to the curb. I was placed in the car and we rode away. I stared at the city thinking to myself I know it's going to be a very long time before I see these streets again, I felt a sense of remorse in my heart that I had never really felt before.

As the sheriff's car headed onto 264, I saw the housing project, Ida Barbour. For the first time it appeared to me how the ground plan was shaped. It would be like a mouse moving through a maze if you walked through trying to find your way out. I had never realized what it looked like from a bird's eye view.

I thought to myself about all the things I had done that was bad in the community with the drug dealing lifestyle. What shame I felt. I could see the young kids on the very same basketball court I once played ball on. Looking down at the innocence I once had, I began to reminisce about the days my brothers and I played on the very same court. I thought about how every Christmas, if you lived in Ida Barbour, you were definitely going to be on the basketball court skating and showing off your new Christmas outfit. I was just caught up in the moment of back in the day and was like in a daydream. Finally after a long ride, we reached our destination.

CHAPTER ELEVEN

DOC: LIFE BEHIND BARS
(Department of Corrections)

Powhatan Correctional Center was my first stop. It reminded me of something like an importing and exporting business. Here, inmates from all over the state of Virginia were being transferred to their next destinations.

I ran into guys I had not seen in years because they were all in prison. We all were being transferred to different buses depending on the assigned location. I was sent to one of Virginia's maximum security prisons, Buckingham Correctional Center. This facility had a reputation for warehousing some of the most dangerous criminals at that time.

Once arriving at the facility I was given the usual orientation, clothing, bed linen, and a rule book. I was then provided a meal and escorted to the sleeping unit where I would be housed. Medical evaluations and the classification process followed. This could sometimes take as long as two to six months depending on how quickly the counselors moved your paperwork.

I was assigned a cell to share with a kat from D.C.

named China Man. He was a street wise dude about my age. He was a light complexioned brother who had slanted eyes. China and I hit it off from the start. He would keep me up all night talking about Alpo Martinez, and Rayful Edmond- two drug kingpins from up North. We would be up all times of night talking about the underworld and drug game legends.

Although I had started reading my bible, I was not totally sold out for Christ and would often entertain my own war stories about my legacy, even sharing the time when I started to dip into my own stash. We would laugh about the Golden rule "never use your own supply". Still being immature I would glorify the operation and the idea that I was down with my folks.

I realized I was slipping back into my old ways when I began to entertain a plan to sell drugs again. I knew I could buy just about anything I wanted on the prison yard. Every weekend kats would just be waiting to see what would be flowing and in circulation for the week.

I began to think about part of that action, I knew it wasn't going to be a good outcome but I still wanted to be in the action. It's a hard cycle to break once you get in that life. I was always told to never try the drug game or the products, because you will like it. The best advice I had ever received before I got trapped into the lifestyle was it doesn't matter whether you are using or dealing, the end result is you are addicted to one or the other leading to a life of incarceration, life setbacks, and eventually death.

There are no winners in the drug game. Most times hustlers end up broke, busted and disgusted. Unless you are a part of cartel which is an entire different level most hustlers are operating from locally.

I had old school dudes coming to me asking if I could get product. I was still sort of fresh from off the streets and my contacts were still doing their thing on the outside. It was just a phone call away. I gave it great thought. I spoke with China Man and moved on it. He had his people in DC, that were willing to come through. The closer it got to making it happen, I would find a way to back out.

I guess my conscious was kicking in. I had been reading my bible and daily devotions. It felt as though the lessons were working. I spoke to my contacts who were willing to supply. China Man had his contacts as well or at least that's what he was telling me. We would put a plan in place that turned out to be disastrous. I talked to an O.G. kat that could help me make some moves. He was well known throughout the prison system. He was definitely one of the most respected guys in the prison system who has a strong faith in Islam. We had done business on the streets, mainly because he was my connection's longtime associate who had married into my family.

My stay was about seven months and I was transferred to another institution - Nottoway Correctional Center. I continued to involve myself in some small time hustling. A part of me wanted change but then another part of me wanted that fast money.

One thing I begin to realize was that prison is like a society. You have to decide what type of life you are going to live there. If you didn't live right while you were in there, you weren't going to live right when you got out. I was my own enemy and it was a mindset that kept me doing the things I was doing. It was a struggle and I had to learn how to get out of my own way.

CHAPTER TWELVE

INDIAN CREEK CORRECTION CENTER

When I arrived at the Indian Creek Correctional Center, sometime in 1994, I had been incarcerated for over four years. To my surprise, they were about to start a therapeutic drug program and were looking for inmates to volunteer to be a part of this therapeutic community.

I began to hate drugs and the life-style that followed it. I remember one day when I had an awakening from this older kat from Florida. He was another one of the O.G's legends. One day he says to me, "Hey young blood," let me holler at you". He began to tell me he knew what I was doing before getting there. He went on to say, that if I didn't stop while I was in prison, I would be right back. He said, "As a matter of fact, it may be a luxury if you make it back", because they are dying every day out there in the streets. I know you don't stand a chance doing right on the outside, so you are going to be right back in here. Oh yea and by the way young blood I got forty years, so I'll be right here when you come back" I went back to my bunk, and I thought about what he had said all that night. The next day a sign-up sheet was going around for volunteers to move into the therapeutic program.

Within days I was one of the first ten guys placed in the therapeutic community. The first building that was structured for the program. Most of my friends begin to joke me and make all sorts of negative comments. I knew I wanted to change, so my response to my friends was "Man it's Over". In my mind I knew if I didn't change now, I would probably die in the streets, or spend the rest of my life behind bars, I was too young for both.

My grandma, who died while I was in the therapeutic program, really made me think about a lot of things she had said to me over the years. Before she passed I had the opportunity to hear her voice over the phone. I told her I had changed my life around and that I was never coming back to jail. I told her I'm back with God now and I'm going to be okay.

I thank God for allowing me to be one of the pioneers for the ICCC Therapeutic Program. While there I was a part of structuring a lot of the community rules, groups and much more. We had an amazing staff, the shaping of this program was phenomenal. I think back on the proudest moment for me, is when I was voted in to be the acting assistant coordinator for the program. Now I know I must have changed. I became a role model for many inmates who had known my history and witnessed the transformation of God in me.

I spent about two years total at the Indian Creek Correctional Center and was transferred to Camp #4 Correctional Center. By now I had been incarcerated for seven years. At this point I had found myself and was living a productive lifestyle within the prison system. Many who knew me, personally or that had met me through my journey from other facilities, were in disbelief of the changes that were taking place in my life.

I continued to attend church on a regular basis. I was witnessing to all my friends about the Lord. Most of them couldn't believe what had taken place in my life. They would keep me under a microscope, but my relationship with the Lord grew closer and closer. I was very active in the prison and spent most of my time serving the Lord in ministry - praying, singing, worshipping with and for other believers.

I had already received my GED and had completed one year of College with NSU. I started working in the kitchen where I fell in love with food service. I would get my little hustle on by making sandwiches and selling them on the yard. I could always count on my homeboy Nuck to gather my orders. He was an old school hustler from back in the day. I know he had a thing for the numbers and would often hit lotto picks winning the earnings of the prison jackpot. He would always have plenty of cigarettes on hand. In prison two things you will learn real fast is that cigarettes is like currency and there was nothing you couldn't get done with them at your demand.

Working in the kitchen gave me access to items like green peppers, onions, cheeses and extra spices. These were hot commodities and a must need for your penitentiary gourmet meal. We used these products to make the famous and favorite meal that was nicknamed (Swoll). Its name came from the oodles of noodles.

At night it was amazing to see what could be created from a bag or two of oodles of noodles. Man, was this a creative idea. You could mix the noodles with tuna or sausages add some cheese, peppers and onions. Mix it all up and you would think you were sitting down at your favorite restaurant. Your side dishes would include crackers and chips. It was a penitentiary delicacy that was enjoyed by everyone. Some prison guards would sneak off with a few crackers topped with the mixture.

While working in the kitchen I would become close with one of the most business savvy brothers of all-time. Morris was from Suffolk. He was my walking buddy. We walked the yard for hours discussing everything from religion, politics and surviving on the outside.

Morris was a true entrepreneur. This guy was a genius and had a strong will to accomplish whatever he put his mind to. There were a few other dudes I considered my buddies that I would hang out with often. My man, Drop, was a very wise, sharp, young dude with the gift of gab. He probably was one of the youngest inmates in all of Camp #4. The old heads really enjoyed Drop's energy and teachable nature. They also liked him because he carried himself with a sense of dignity. We all knew that when Drop got out, he would probably never return if he applied what he knew in a positive way.

Then there was this other dude that fascinated us with his knowledge. We called him Pop. He was a very intellectual brother who had graduated from Virginia State University. He was the brother with the education and street smarts. What we all really liked about Pop is that although he was educated, he was still very down to earth.

I was certain that the conversation from these dudes would take us down another path. There were a few other dudes I would kick it with often about various topics. You had people from all types of backgrounds with many talents and gifts. There was always something to be learned.

CHAPTER THIRTEEN

A NEW MINDSET

For as a man thinketh in his heart, so is he.
Proverbs 23:7 (KJV)

My first prison job I started working was in the dish room. I was always networking with the old timers who ran the kitchen. It always seemed that prison cooks had a sense of entitlement among the kitchen staff and others at least it appeared that way. So me, with my entrepreneur mind, saw this as a long term investment and a potential career possibility to take back to the outside life. Working in a kitchen was something far better than dealing drugs which was no longer my reality.

I worked hard to get connected to the cooks. This old timer "Fat Man" from the Manor –my homie would be my link to the kitchen manager. I went to speak with Fats and he said in his very cool and calm voice, "I got you Mike!"He talked to the food service manager to get me a position as a cook or baker.

I don't know what he said to him, but the next week I was moved to the bake shop straight from out of the tray room washing dishes. This was considered a huge accomplishment in prison. We had pay scales and I left from an unskilled job making .20 cents an hour to a skilled job making .35cents an hour. That was a big deal!

I had no skills at all and was introduced to this brother from Newport News named Ant. He was a prized baker and knew his stuff. He was one of the best bakers in the prison system. He gave me what I needed to get started. From there my skills increased and I became so good that I was promoted to head baker. This promotion increased my pay to .45 cents an hour.

I enrolled in the apprenticeship baking class and completed that course receiving my journeymen's card. I became well known for my baking skills. I stayed on camp # 4 for three years. My next transfer was to St. Brides Correctional Center. By now I had been in prison for over 10 years.

After arriving at St. Brides Correctional Center, I got off the prison bus and saw so many old friends and associates that I hadn't seen in many years. It felt like I was at a reunion. After getting settled, my first stop was to the kitchen to apply for a job. I was hired on the spot as the head baker. The word had traveled that I was an excellent baker and with an apprenticeship card it was pretty much a done deal.

I began to work and prove myself to the kitchen staff. I was promoted to the assistant cook. I enrolled once again into another apprenticeship program as a cook this time. Before finishing the program, the kitchen staff asked me to be the head cook. I later successfully completed a three year apprenticeship cooking program.

I was actively involved in most of the programs at St. Bride's. Many of the inmates were much younger than me. I became known as sort of that model inmate. I had a very small circle of people I would associate with. My homeboy Jack "O" and I was real close, that was my partner. We could always have us a productive conversation on just about anything. He was a very intellectual old timer that would often time educate me on the world of politics, this dude was real sharp and always kept me laughing. We became good friends. I was often chosen by the administration staff to participate in many rehabilitation programs. I began to facilitate the N/A program and started another peer support group for young guys with one of the counselors.

I was even chosen to be the head Coordinator in the kitchen and supervised the entire inmate staff. In my spare time I went to the library every day. There I started learning more about computers. I taught myself with the help of the librarian, Mr. Pic who was an older Caucasian man very small in stature, but bold and feisty. Mr. Pic loved books the way most people love money, he would repair damage books as though he was doing wound care. He showed me a lot and prepared me to actually run the entire library. He taught me everything about computers and books.

I would go on to be offered a job as the library Aid. This required me to resign from my job as the Kitchen Coordinator. It was an emotional time for me because of the healthy relationships I built with most of the staff and kitchen inmate workers. After all I had spent more time in the kitchen than I did in my own cell block. My job as the library clerk involved me running Follett, a software program that is used to organize, and maintain books, videos and other items that are in circulation by the public. It was a sad day for me when Mr. Pic decided to call it quits. His last day at work he gave me the longest speech ever which was well received, we both begin to tear up as we said our final good-bye.

I became so knowledgeable about my job that when Mr. Pic retired I was asked to work with the new Librarian by the DCE Principal. This was an honor. Mr. Owens took over the library then we became very close during my last three years of incarceration. A lot happened beyond my control, but Mr. Owens and others helped me through some hard times. I lost my baby sister to breast cancer and my son's mother passed away RIP(Faye Gatling). I was devastated.

After seeing many inmates leave the prison system only to return within a few years and in some cases within months always made me think about my own life. Time was running out and I was about to exit those same doors.

My ninety day countdown was right around the corner. The reality of my change was about to be tested and I was becoming a bit nervous. My mind began to race with thoughts of not wanting the plight of my past to become my identity.

CHAPTER FOURTEEN

NINETY DAY COUNT DOWN

Everybody would remind me by saying "hey you are getting short man" although I felt like I was prepared, there was still a lot to consider. I was thinking about how I was going to get that first job with no transportation, housing was not going to be a problem, but was it going to be a healthy environment? Would I have a supportive Parole Officer? Who will help me? What about all the fines, court cost, child support and arrearage money I owed? Those were the questions that baffled my intellect.

Amongst most of these concerns I knew I was blessed because I didn't have to worry about the same dysfunctional conditions some returning citizens would have to face because the difference was I had a great support system. Most would return to the long history of drug abuse and drug dealing environments. And some had no self identification. I know all odds are against most, but my logic became at least I have more than the twenty-five dollars an offender gets when leaving prison to establish a new life. I had saved money every chance I got. I had so much to consider, but with only ninety days to go, reality quickly began to set in and I had to be ready.

My new reality was now classified as a matter of life or death so to speak, because one wrong move and it was back behind the prison walls. Most institutional release plans mainly consisted of a home plan with a verifiable address that one would be residing at. I only had a few days before I was going to be a free man. I still worried if I would make it or if I could survive on the outside, because so many others didn't but I vowed to be the exception that did.

Unbeknownst to me I became a role model for others to emulate in prison and also a master of doing well behind bars. Now, I had to apply all that I had learned on the inside to the outside world. I know some people in society are not in the business of welcoming felons home; however, I knew I had a plan. I was released from prison after thirteen years and I was ready to go out and start my life over.

I often thought it would have been nice if there was a program in place to help guide me back into society when I was released from prison. There was clearly a demonstrated need for a comprehensive mentoring program that could help returning citizens prepare for release back into their communities. This concept would potentially reduce the recidivism rate greatly by helping those returning citizens stay committed to their new life's goals.

CHAPTER FIFTEEN

STARTING ALL OVER AGAIN

Then Jesus said, "Come to me, all of you who are weary and carry heavy burdens, and I will give you rest. Matt 11:28(KJV)

Due to the nature of my charges I was assigned to one of the most stern Parole Officers in the city of Chesapeake. Everyone was telling me that he was a no-nonsense probation officer. The first time I met him I saw what everyone was talking about but contrary to those thoughts I convinced myself that we would become the best of friends.

I just kept speaking God's word to myself. I had a made up mind that going backwards to a lifestyle of drugs and crime was not an option for me. I was speaking those things that were not as though they were so they would come to pass. I was standing on God to go before me and prepare my way.

I attended my scheduled meetings faithfully while contributing to group discussions as much as possible. It wasn't long before my parole officer began asking me to speak at group meetings at other facilities. He saw my commitment and dedication and eventually he asked me to speak at a Probation and Parole substance abuse meeting.

The day of the event we met at my apartment and rode to the prison in South Hampton County. I had no idea what I was going to say. Every passing moment seemed to be intense. By the time we reached the prison, I knew exactly what my speech would be. I felt God's presence with me as the words flowed from my heart, and the message was simple. God said remind them and encourage them to seek me first. I left there feeling lifted myself.

Mr. Owens was a very wise and observant man who kept a close watch on his library aids and that's not to say it was due to a lack of trust, but in a prison environment I'm sure all of the staff are trained not to trust inmates. Mr. Owens was retired from the Military and I'm sure he was prepared to deal with the best of con men behind the prison walls. I had established a good rapport with him over the years that I had worked for him so much so, that he advocated on my behalf to get me my first job. He personally went to NSU and presented my situation to them which ultimately lead to my first working opportunity. The very first week I was released Mr. Owens had an interview set up for me, I was blessed to get hired as a cook earning top pay with full benefits, now that was God! My next hurdle would be transportation issues. I was willing to do whatever I had to do to get to work. My brother and sister would often times provide support with transportation whenever they could. After ninety days on the job with a perfect attendance record my supervisor was so impressed with my work performance and commitment that he vowed to give me a raise and help me purchase a vehicle. I had recently paid off all of my fines and had my license reinstated. I had a simple plan which consisted of me going to work, church, and the gym.

I arrived at work one morning and my supervisor called me in his office, he said I've been thinking and I have a car at my house and it doesn't need much work. If you're interested I will sell you the car and all I'm asking is for five hundred dollars down and the other five hundred you can pay bi-weekly until the debt is settled. I was overcome by emotions for the first time in a long time. I knew God was with me. I had prayed and said lord if you bless me with another chance I will never sell drugs again and I'm elated to say that I've kept my promise.

Life was going good. I felt like I could breathe a little and I was moving on up. From out of nowhere I received a letter from child support to pay the interest that had accumulated over the years and I'm talking in the tens of thousands of dollars. I was threatened about jail one time if I didn't pay. I made arrangements to have the money taken out of my check so I would not overlook this bill. The case worker I was assigned to was very generous and helped me work through this matter.

I was always taught that if I was faithful to God, he would be faithful to me. I received a promotion which meant more money. The lord was showing me in so many ways that he was there for me. There were so many good and positive things happening. I received a call from Mr. Owens asking me if I would be the guest speaker for the graduation at St. Brides Correctional Center. I was amazed and humbled and accepted the invitation. I seized the opportunity to use this as a platform to reverence God's purpose and plan for my life because this is what I was created for. I remember feeling that my life was really being turned around for my good and God's glory!

I continued working at NSU and was promoted again to head cook for the staff dining hall which serves the professors and the public. This was a major accomplishment by the standards of the entire management team. While working in this position I met another cook who always talked about the Urban League.

I had no clue whatsoever about this organization or what they did. He would always say they helped low income people and they also worked within the community helping adults and youth with a lot of services. The first chance I got, I looked at their information online and was eager to learn more. I went into the office and was greeted by the receptionist. She asked me a few questions and all I remember is speaking with her about volunteering. I had always said when I was released from prison I would give back to the communities that I once helped to tear down.

I took that opportunity to volunteer and was trained to teach a mini life skill training course for a summer youth program. They had a contract with the City Of Norfolk. I reported to the site to volunteer and I didn't realize I would be preparing a classroom full of high school students for a summer employment experience, after all I had worked for something similar when I was a teen.

After finishing the class, which in my opinion went well the students were instructed to evaluate their facilitator. To my surprise, the students obliviously gave me an outstanding report and wanted me to return the following year. I continued volunteering with the Urban League for a few years. I went from doing general duties to job development and learning how to do case management. The Urban League was inadvertently preparing me for a different career. Never did I ever imagine the phenomenal things that were awaiting me on the other side in spite of all the things I had done in my past.

I was preparing for summer break as we normally did yearly. This was the time of year when working at NSU was the least favorite part of the job because students would be leaving for break which meant work would slow down on campus forcing most food service workers to apply for unemployment benefits. It was a blessing receiving it, but in all reality it wasn't enough to maintain my overall living expenses. I would always find myself struggling to make ends meet but I still continued to fulfill my volunteering obligation with the Urban League.

In my search for more opportunities I once went to The Second Chances Program that was mentioned to me by a very close friend. I didn't meet the eligibility requirements for the program but was given pertinent information on the Step Up Program, who also provided services for ex-offenders.

In mid June I received a call from the Urban League in regards to a possible case manager position working with the VIEW Program (Virginia Initiative for Employment not Welfare). She wanted to know if I was interested. Before she could get the words out of her mouth, I said I'll take it!

She provided me with a gentleman's name to call and instructed me to tell him that the Urban League had referred me. I spoke with the gentleman during a lengthy interview and within three days I was reporting to the Social Services building in Downtown Norfolk. I was in disbelief. After all this was Social Services, I was thinking could this really be happening?

The Director and I had a very interesting conversation. I explained my situation to him, including my background. I told him I would not disappoint him if he gave me a chance and he did. I had landed my first job working in a professional environment. I was still in a state of shock but that quickly transitioned to a vast amount of gratitude. I knew it was the Lord working on my behalf.

My caseload went from five people during my training period to over one hundred participants. I was very excited about my job which eventually paved the path for what was to come in my future for many years. The director was very impressed about my passion to help others.

One of my most memorable moments was the day

I was recognized by Human Services, Probation and Parole, and my Director for my service to an elderly gentleman. As a result, I received a "You Make A Difference Award" It was the best day of my life to have accomplished something of that magnitude. I had no expectations of receiving any recognition. I went to work every day trying to help the participants in the program.

The stories I would hear on a daily basis often sent me home with a hurting heart. I worked hard to be the best case manager I knew how to be. I wanted to leave a positive impact on everyone that I encountered. The implied mission was to leave them with a message of hope.

Cynthia Thompson, was hired as our new Assistant Director for the VIEW program. From the very beginning I thought she would be a great fit for the team, she appeared to have the passion, strength and the right temperament for the job. This was no easy position to manage by any means. I witnessed her step into her role like only she could. In my opinion she was that driving force that was needed to bring about a change of team spirit. She managed to transform the entire atmosphere of the team.

She was fair and always operated with a spirit of excellence, while displaying this burst of positivity that was infectious to all whom she encountered. I learned later that she previously came from an agency that worked with ex-offenders.

As time passed our working relationship grew closer to the point where I felt comfortable enough to share my life's journey with her. I began to tell her more and more about my personal life. I told her things that nobody else knew about me other than the Director. I don't know why I said to her one day, if you was to ever leave the program don't forget about me, because I would like to work with the Second Chances Program should you go back, keep in mind I had no idea she was planning on leaving.

At this point in time I had made a conscious decision to inquire about becoming a Certified Substance Abuse Counselor (CSAC-A). One day at work one of my co-workers was talking about a certification program that was being offered. I then began my journey to becoming certified as a CSAC-A. I started out by enrolling in school at Tidewater Community College and then transferring all of my credits to Liberty University. That road to getting my CSAC-A was not easy due to my previous background. My certification was actually denied the first time and I had to jump through a lot of bureaucratic hoops prior to receiving the certification.

After a long battle, I was told I couldn't possess that type of certification even though I had successfully completed all the requirements. After all I was a former convicted felon. I was instructed that I needed to arrange an appointment to talk with the Department of Health Professions in Richmond. They would be responsible for authorizing such licensure.

It took several attempts before I finally received a hearing date. I was asked to state to the board why I should be allowed to possess a certification as a Substance Abuse Counselor. So I begin to tell my story from beginning to end. I had shared and answered all their questions. I was asked to step out of the room as they made their final decision.

I waited around forty-five minutes to an hour praying as I waited. Finally the big decision had come down. I was called back to the room and they began to read all these Virginia codes, the way they do in court room proceedings. A few more questions were asked and to my surprise the Executive Director asked me a personal question about my own sobriety, which I adamantly stated, "I have not had any involvement with selling or using drugs in any capacity in over twenty years." She then asked me "What was your recovery plan for putting your life back together? How did you change your life?" I replied, "Ma'am, I found Jesus when I was in prison and my life has never been the same again." They all just stared at me and then the proceeding continued. She went around the room to poll the board. Everybody had voted in support of me getting my certification. She said, "I would like to dismiss this board and just speak with Mr. Marshall off the record". She began to tell me that everything I said really touched her personally. She went on to share that she was a recovering addict and she believed that I was going to go on to help a lot of people. She advised me to stick to my plan because it has worked so well for me. She forewarned me of the risk of relapse due to stress. In closing she reminded me that if she could ever be of assistance to me, feel free to contact her. And I've never forgotten those kind words. I thanked her and left the room with peace and contentment in my heart knowing that once again, the Lord had gone before me and interceded on my behalf.

That was the defining moment in my life where I surrendered completely. I began to worship in spirit while exclaiming repentance in my heart for all of my short comings throughout my life's course. Immediately I experienced this indescribable feeling that engulfed my presence and my life has soared from that moment to this one. And in spite of all the odds that were stacked up against me. I had now defied those odds and achieved something that people said I could not do. That is the best feeling in the world to know that you are an over comer!

We have all been afforded different life chances and throughout my journey as a professional I've learned to meet people right where they are. Change is something that inherently takes place over time. The likelihood of an overnight success story is slim to none on the average. So therefore, one must first identify with their own issues, problems, or concerns and make the necessary changes as desired.

All human interaction begins with a thought and the mind is the core of making those thoughts occur. Although, everyone's perception will not be the same we have to respect each individual's choice. It would not be a wise decision to continue making inappropriate choices with the expectation of obtaining a different outcome. There has to be a substantial deposit in order to make a withdrawal!

It is imperative that we take the time to lead by example and teach on the premise that one never has to be a product of any negative environment, but we have to be willing to help bridge the gap. I'm a living testament of that, and I'm still standing by the grace of God and today I continue to work with those individuals that need a **First Opportunity** in life. It's an honor to serve and help those individuals that the Lord will continue to put in my path.

CHAPTER SIXTEEN

LIFE AFTER PRISON

City Hall –Second Chances Program

God gave me my life back after prison. Everything that has been shared was not for me, but brought forth to encourage others to know that if they believe it, they can achieve it. I was broken but never cast out because I know someone with a loving redemptive power that is far greater than any of my circumstances. Anything worth having is worth fighting for and the ultimate purpose of this book is not to glorify any crime, not to tell war stories or anything of its kind, but rather to be a voice of hope for whatever your journey has been or continues to be.

"Once Upon A Time" situations can evolve from numerous chain of events including but not limited to homelessness, domestic violence, incarceration,

113

drugs, addiction, divorce, obesity, homosexuality, gambling, promiscuity, or whatever the issue may be.

As the years have gone by one would think that this cyclical response would have ended. I have seen the pain and devastation in the face's of many parents. I see the hopelessness in the eyes of our young people. My heart aches for the solution to this epidemic of black on black killings. Some days when I read the newspaper or watch the news, I'm reminded about how far we have to go to eradicate this trajectory of destruction that is claiming the lives of innocent people as well. My heart goes out to the mothers and fathers who are losing their sons and daughters to senseless murders every day.

One must understand that there can be restoration after a fall. The aftermath can be as great as one want it to be, but this requires dedication to the craft of time management. This process includes evaluating, planning, and implementing your ideas in a way that will bring about the desired transformation. Modifications may consist of changing ones environment, associates, and lifestyle to promote new healthier life choices without incidence.

My mere existence has been blessed beyond measure. If someone had told me my life would be this way today I wouldn't have believed it. My relationship with my children is so much healthier than before. The bond that I have with my only son, who I love dearly is now stronger which took some time to build, but it's definitely a blessing in disguise to feel the love reciprocated from him today. The bond that I have with my daughter continues to flourish and I am so proud of her. She is a graduate from ODU's Psychology Program and is currently working with vulnerable populations including youth and adults.

Things have been changing so rapidly for me over the past few years and my assignments as well as my territory seems to be increasing. The Second Chances Program would go through a period of transitioning and staffing.

During this process I was promoted to Acting Vice President of the Program. I served in this role for a relatively short period of time but the experience and exposure that I gained will be with me for a lifetime. It changed my professional career forever. I had gone from being a case manager of the program to the Acting Vice President under the STOP Organization. I was in a position of leadership that I never saw coming. I was confident that God wasn't putting me anywhere that he hadn't prepared me to be. Some people didn't have the confidence in me and I knew it, but I stayed on the right path with a level head and calmness and watched God work through me.

I've had the privilege to sit on various discussion panels as it relates to re-entry which includes educational entities such as NSU, TCC, and ODU. All participation was by invitation from re-entry professionals to serve on their diverse forums. I was promoted by upper management several times and had not once sought out a position on my own.

I know God's favor was upon me and still is because I couldn't have made any of this happen on my own. There were times when I felt like I didn't deserve anything. After all, I had failed so many times in life. The Lord was keeping me. And there were also times when I honestly wanted to give up. I couldn't understand and my question was why me Lord? When in all actuality I should have been saying why not me?

I left prison owing over $17,000 in child support. I thought I could never resolve this debt. However, God said I could and I was able to resolve all of my debt with child support. It seemed impossible to get a zero balance but I did.

Ms. Thompson, the Director of the program at the time and myself had been discussing putting on a production that would highlight the plight of returning citizens from incarceration as a means of fundraising. So we talked to Allen Ellis, who's a local producer of stage plays to consult with us on this project.

We had ninety days to get this accomplished. I began to write this story about my life not knowing at the time it would become the framework for my book. I began day by day organizing my thoughts and key points about the story I was trying to tell. After all, a lot had happened and there were so many things I had forgotten. What I realized was that as I began to write the story my memory started coming back to me.

I spent about four hours a night working on this writing. I became frustrated and often times had feelings of anger, sadness, and shame of all the things that had happened in my life. I kept writing and the more I wrote the better I began to feel. For once in my life I allowed the feelings that were buried deep down inside of me to be released.

Finally, my writing was now completed but I realized I had written it in a way that probably only I could understand it. I found myself going back to re-type all that I had written. Keep in mind I can only type a small percentage of words per minute. I was really struggling but I was determined that I was going to finish this project on time. I was given a deadline that I had to adhere to because everything was riding on the story I was writing.

I remember the morning I finished. It was such a relief. It was now the big day. Ms. Thompson and myself would meet with Allen, to discuss my writing. We met downtown at City Hall. We started the meeting with a prayer and immediately began to discuss the strategy for the play. Mr. Allen and I went back and forth discussing minor details about the different events in my life story. He was finding it hard to write as a play and would eventually suggest that this sounds like a book. However, the play was a success and we had a great turn out.

My employment with Second Changes opened many opportunities for me to be seated on various committees and panels which has allowed me to speak to a diverse group of professionals. I have been involved with Norfolk Re-entry Council that consists of many agencies that address the needs of formally incarcerated individuals. I have also worked with Norfolk Re-entry Court that works with offenders who have been screened to participate in a program that offers an alternative to incarceration.

My future goals consists of my continuance to serve my fellow constituents by helping to create a new beginning for others. Ultimately, I'm very interested in ascertaining a Bachelor's Degree in Psychology from Regent University to help me create a newfound Once Upon A Time Journey.

APPENDIX

I receive a great deal of mail from prisons yearly. This letter was actually written by a good friend from my childhood. Receiving letters such as these is what gives me the motivation to continue the journey of advocating for others who are where, I was in my past.

Michael Marshall

4/2/15

Hello Mike,

How you doing for starter? Well as for me I'm still hanging in there maintaining making good out of a bad situation, but other than that I'm holding my own staying out of trouble.

Mike I would've been wrote you but I misplace your address the one you gave me when you came up here when your brother was here.

Oh! By the way tell him and Tony that I said hello, and for the both of them to continue to stay focus. Also tell Tony he deserve his freedom he did his, and to keep it stay out of harm way.

Also give the rest of your family my love as well, may God be with you all.

Mike I mean this what I'm about to say, I'm very proud of you Bro. I mean that from the bottom of my heart you're definitely an inspiration one I definitely look up to. You been through this all that I'm going through but yet you manage to make something out yourself which I respect to the fullest. Keep doing what your doing because it's working. I love you man with my heart and soul more then you'll ever know.

You always where my mind... most even when we use to hang together back in the days. I'm asking you, not ashamed to do so, give me the game, I need your help. I'm tired of doing my time, I'm burned out. I feel as though I'm ready to take on other challenges of my life, I still feel that life has alot to offer me. I also know that I have to put in the work just as you have done, and I'm willing.

So continue to succeed in life, thank god continuously for your blessing always because he is the way, the truth, and the light. I love you Boo. I will be calling you soon at your office number (252) 627-8686 or your fax number 395-9136.

TAKE CARE

PA TEN

121

INCARCERATION STATS

- US has 2.3 million people incarcerated
- 680,000 People released from prison in this country each year
- Incarceration costs continue to rise. State spending for corrections reached $52.4 billion in fiscal year 2012 -2014 and has been higher
- The Department of Justice estimates that states and the federal government combined spends $80 billion on corrections yearly
- 2 out 3 inmates are rearrested in 3- years.
- Virginia Prison Population is between 37,000 - 38,000
- Average age is 36.5 years old
- 49% entered without a High School education, or GED
- 85% has a document history of drugs and Alcohol Abuse
- Virginia release about 12,000 offenders annually

REFERENCES

http://www.bop.gov/

http://www.casacolumbia.org/

http://www.nasbo.org/

http://www.vadoc.virginia.gov/

http://www.vera.org/services/research

Made in the USA
Middletown, DE
17 June 2022

67344809R00071